I0417610

PRACTICE THE ART TO LOVE

Course Program Level 1
Course 1.1: Practice the Art to Love

With theses and exercises: Relationship, sex and love,
partnership, being a woman and being a man,
renewal, searching a partner, choosing a partner,

REALIZE YOUR DREAMS AND VISIONS FOR LOVE!

LOVE YOURSELF AND TAKE HAPPINESS INTO YOUR OWN HANDS!

CREATE HONEST RELATIONSHIPS WITH PLEASURE, FUN AND JOY!

CIRCUMSPECTLY SATISFY YOUR DESIRES AND NEEDS!

USE KNOWLEDGE, WISDOM AND SKILLS FOR LIVING!

5

Lesson 1
Create your relationship in manifold ways

12

Lesson 2
Discover being a woman and being a man

20

Lesson 3
Love and love yourself completely

26

Lesson 4
Enjoy making love with creativity

35

Lesson 5
Live your relationship partnership-like

42

Lesson 6
Prepare yourself well for love

This distance learning training program is the preparation for all kind of solutions. Here you find a lot of suggestions to live love. The aims: to find a clearer view in relationship matters; to recognize thoroughly your situation for love; to precisely understand critical situations; to develop autonomy with efficient solutions; to prepare best possible changes of critical situations. Love is wonderful! Prepare yourself for such a gift of love! Form yourself for love! Practice the art to love, enjoy love and the love for life!

- By reading the exercises you will adapt knowledge for living.
- By doing the exercises you will recognize yourself.
- By contemplating your result, you will start changing yourself.
- By changing yourself you broaden yourself and grow widely.
- By understanding your being, you find your happiness and your fulfillment.

SCHELLHAMMER INSTITUTE
IN SOMNIS VERITAS

Make more with your being and life!

Knowledge is power! Incomprehension means powerlessness! Most people know less than 3-5% about their psychical-spiritual being and life. They are at the mercy of the unknown rest. That's like a captain who is aware of 3-5% of his ship and of the conditions of the passage; to the rest he is blindly exposed. Such navigation must be a nightmare and will surely lead to a catastrophe.

And you, dear reader, you are the captain of your being and life. Where will this lead if you don't know 95-97% of your being and life and if you don't control it? Wake up and live with open eyes!

A saying: Life is the school for a young adult, discharged from school. But what does life teach people? Do they learn what is really necessary from their life for the personal success and happiness in relationships and self-fulfillment?

Fact is that most people do not learn enough from their life. With that we come to the point: What is essential in learning? Open your eyes and you will quickly see!

If you never learn about yourself in life, about your way of living, about your partner, about your relationships, about sex, about love and a lot more, at the end of your life you basically sacrifice your evolutionary chances. Your human being remains unconscious and archaic.

Everybody makes mistakes in life, has failures, difficulties, crisis, pains, and fails even during years in everything. That's life and that's "normal". The real problem starts when people don't learn; don't acquire knowledge and skills for living. Consequently, one produces for oneself a life with little consciousness.

Failure, crisis and suffering contain chances: with oneself and one's life to achieve higher aims. Do you want to stick your head into the sand and simply look away? Wake up and live, but correctly!

The problem gets even worse if a person rejects knowing himself, educating himself, changing himself, growing and developing himself. That's certainly a self-evident pre-condition for all good aims concerning relationships, sex, love, partnership, being a woman/man, renewing one's life, looking for a partner, etc.

If man doesn't develop himself consciously from his inner being aiming higher quality of being, life forces him to be and to become what the external world forces him to be and to become.

You have the choice: ignorant or clever? Wake up and look at reality! And learn! Think and act corresponding realities. That means: "living correctly"!

The particular joy of life starts when man can dedicate himself to life and at the same time take into his hands his human being and life successfully.

With the necessary knowledge of life and a lot of practical exercises you can build up your success in a relationship, in ways of creating life and self-fulfillment with this educational program.

This is the path to love and happiness. Practice the art to love and love yourself!

Dr. Edward Schellhammer

© SCHELLHAMMER INSTITUTE

Create your relationship in manifold ways

Thesis 1

In a relationship two human beings are face to face with each other. Both have a complex psychical life. There are multiple causes that produce tensions and conflicts. Everybody can clarify them. Everybody can grow through that. There are several initial stages to improve the quality of a relationship.

☑ Exercise 1
Mark what is right for you.

☐ There are a few things going on in my mind I don't understand well.

☐ My biography is rather charged and still has effects on me.

☐ Certain expressions in front of my partner are not constructive.

☐ Certain patterns of behavior in relation to my partner are not well reflected.

☐ My social system (relatives, friends) weigh down my relationship.

☐ I don't have a strongly marked life style in living together.

☐ Sometimes a "shadow" from me breaks through and then a quarrel escalates.

☐ I have certain small and bigger complexes that disturb certain situations.

☐ I have a certain tendency to provoke confrontations.

☐ I have a lack of knowledge and skills for life and relationship.

☐ The development of my personality is rather hindered in my relationship.

☐ I can't really live my nature (character as a man/woman).

What do you conclude from that for yourself? ....

....

....

....

....

....

....

....

....

....

         © SCHELLHAMMER INSTITUTE

Thesis 2 — Many hopes are connected in a relationship between man and woman: peace, joy, harmony, fulfillment, desire tenderness, love, eroticism, good sex, care, constructive communication, faithfulness, safety, etc. This and much more we can find partnership-like linked with attitudes and behavior.

☐ ☑ **Exercise 2**
☑ ☐ What have you experienced only slightly or not at all from the following partnership-like principles in your relationship? Mark what is important to you.

☐ Mutual respect of the different nature (character, expression, gender).
☐ Reciprocity and equality in all life areas.
☐ Alternating nearness and distance in living together.
☐ Understanding about the differences and common interests.
☐ Respecting the limits of the other and the world of the other.
☐ In communication, the daily life gets a consciously cared central space.
☐ Stimulating love through small attentions.
☐ No mutual balancing of the mistakes and the undeveloped aspects.
☐ Reason and intelligence are supportive functions in all concerns.
☐ Eroticism, being in love and seduction has a place in the usual daily life.
☐ A high level of self-management (life techniques) on both sides.
☐ Acceptance of tensions, conflicts and certain risks.
☐ Mutual acceptance and fulfillment of sexual desire with love.
☐ Skills and effort to understand the partner and life in general.
☐ A constructive care of the "inner child" and the weaknesses.
☐ Mutually creating (developing) of femininity and masculinity.
☐ Resolving together objective matters, interests and aims.
☐ Distribution of roles is discussed and accepted; but remains flexible.

What do you conclude from that for yourself? ....

....

....

....

....

....

....

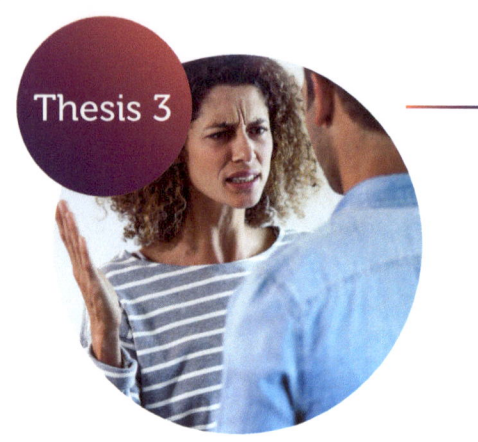

Thesis 3 —— A successful resolution of conflicts in the relationship demands skills to love and social competences (life techniques).

Exercise 3

Manifold situations arise in the daily life of a relationship that give motive to quarrel. Mark what produces arguments and conflicts in your relationship.

Mark what concerns you / what is important to you: **1 = not 2 = little 3 = quite a lot 4 = a lot 5 = totally**

1	2	3	4	5	
☐	☐	☐	☐	☐	Not expressing clearly and concretely one's own needs.
☐	☐	☐	☐	☐	Misunderstandings even in small concerns because of unclear talks.
☐	☐	☐	☐	☐	Ignoring something to avoid a possible argument.
☐	☐	☐	☐	☐	Not giving seriousness to one's own feelings and the ones of the partner.
☐	☐	☐	☐	☐	Talking in unsuitable moments and situations about important matters.
☐	☐	☐	☐	☐	Not planning / deciding timely what is important and urgent.
☐	☐	☐	☐	☐	Eating, drinking and watching TV because of frustration or boredom.
☐	☐	☐	☐	☐	Behaving aggressively to create distance or to drive out (suppress).
☐	☐	☐	☐	☐	Unpunctuality practiced secretly in order to manipulate.
☐	☐	☐	☐	☐	Disorderliness indirectly expressing a protest or a provocation.
☐	☐	☐	☐	☐	Dissatisfaction as a result of a lack of common life aims.
☐	☐	☐	☐	☐	Financial problems / differences in dealing with money (consumption).
☐	☐	☐	☐	☐	Neglecting sexual desires (one's own and the ones of the partner).
☐	☐	☐	☐	☐	Carelessness, coldness, rudeness, negligence, indifference.

What do you conclude from that for yourself? ....

....

....

....

....

Thesis 4

To get success in a relationship first a common base is needed, love and ability to love; but (self-) education is also necessary: self-knowledge, knowledge about human being, forming personality, life learning and the process of Individuation.

Exercise 4
Find new views and attitudes. Mark what is necessary or especially important to you in the daily dealing with relationship problems:

☐ Talking together is a learning process; e.g. through thinking about talking.
☐ There is no partnership without strong arguments sometimes.
☐ Some arguments hide a deficit of life skills and self-education.
☐ Arguing about banalities arises because of a deficit of conscious self-control.
☐ The total harmony doesn't exist! It's a serious problem if one is seeking for it.
☐ Frustration with one's self converts to a frustration in the relationship.
☐ Dogmas and ideologies are poison for a relationship with self-fulfillment.
☐ Many problems in a relationship have a lot to do with the whole person.
☐ Resolving relationship problems often demands also growth of the person.
☐ Learning and educational processes (reading, courses, etc.) are indispensable.

What do you conclude from that for yourself? ....
....
....
....

Exercise 5
My most important relationship problems are:

1...................................   4...................................   7...................................

2...................................   5...................................   8...................................

3...................................   6...................................   9...................................

Exercise 6
That's the way I want to resolve my relationship problems now: ....
....
....
....

Self-being through a Relationship

The expectations of a relationship are enormous. The sufferings and difficulties in many relationships speak volumes. Human beings wish for harmony, love, happiness, tenderness, joy, fulfillment and peace through being together.

Longing for love, for being in love, eroticism and lust experiences cause a quantity of illusions and hopes which nearly all crumble away over the years.

Many 'stable' relationships fail. It may be better not to judge this. Mainly it isn't adequate to speak about 'guilt'. If we take 'failure' as a critical category, then everywhere people are failing with mostly worse consequences. One can also fail in a 'single'-life. This happens as often!

If we reduce the intensity of well-being feelings, maybe longing or maybe intimate experiences, then we have two people who feel a deep mutual sympathy and estimation. Both have a complex psychical life. Both have a biography with nearly infinite conditioned images and experiences.

The life history of both contains a lot of disordered, unelaborated and connected elements. Both live in a social system - family, acquaintances, and friends, colleagues - in a specific cultural environment and in a working world. Both have their habits, their behavior patterns, their talents, their antipathies towards things, human beings and attitudes. Both have an individual body-relation, an individual lust-experience, habits of eating and clothing, habits of movement, a kind of care for the body and a relation to nature and animals.

A huge amount of beliefs, attitudes and small values stay combined or in contradiction. Also feelings, psycho-dynamism and biorhythm are different. Finally there is also an indissoluble genuine difference between man and woman.

Disappointments, collusions, neurotic development, quarrels, conflicts and even psycho-somatic reactions are preconditioned. Many people try to protect their 'bastion' with religious attitudes or with clever self-deception.

There are many 'arrangements' which sometimes appear as the only solution. The answer for conflicts in relationship isn't psychotherapy! Except if one is indeed psychically ill.

We can only see what we know or that which we are attentive to; for example: the unconscious effects of the biography, the variety of the psychical needs, the ability of the force of love.

The one who doesn't take his psychical forces seriously, neither forms his self-management with a clear view nor trains mental fitness, cannot see these realities in his life partner. And he cannot offer a constructive communication and solutions for these subjects.

1. A relationship has to be linked with self-realization, if it is to stand a chance.

2. Education is necessary: Self-knowledge, human-knowledge, personality-education.

In a relationship without psychical education, sooner or later the repetitions
of the individual experiences from the childhood come up:

- imitating mother (as woman)
- imitating father (as man)
- repeating parental patterns of quarrelling
- parental punishing
- effects of super-ego, formed in childhood
- linked to familiar patterns of value
- repetition of typical daily patterns
- imitating the language of the parents

- reactivation of early relation to the parents
- make up for earlier trials to break free
- trying to satisfy deficits from childhood
- make up for the unfinished puberty
- anxiety about being separated from parents
- style of parental talk at the table
- patterns of conflict concerning house work
- flight to mother/father (as protection)

SELF-REALIZATION THROUGH PERSONALITY EDUCATION AND INDIVIDUATION IS A PRECONDITION FOR A SUCCESSFUL RELATIONSHIP.

A partnership-relation (married life) is a kind of living, with mutual understanding and participation with the aim to realize this human being together. Having and educating children, the creation of a new family life can be a chance to reflect individual experiences, to work them out and to live new forms with self-education:

- to integrate the partner into one's self-education (communication, participation)
- to realize oneself and to do everything so that the partner can also realize himself
- to form one's own masculinity (femininity) in the psyche through the partner
- to increase the force of love to find out the 'mystery of life' together

You want to know more, more examples and more practical ideas to this unit.
These books from Dr. Edward Schellhammer guide you for much more:

Love your Life

The Future in your Hands

Become a strong Personality

60 Days to Paradise

Practical Psychology

Lesson 2

Discover being a woman and being a man

© SCHELLHAMMER INSTITUTE

Thesis 1

Man and woman are naturally (substantially) different:

- The psychical life (mind) as a whole doesn't work equally with men and women.

- Female and male roles are not all simply products of learning processes.

- Femininity and masculinity are psychological and biological qualities.

- No man (woman) becomes a man (woman) without the opposite gender.

- Man and woman have the psychical opposite gender as a polarity in their psyche (known as "anima" and "animus").

Exercise 1
Overloaded experiences. Mark what affects you.

☐ I have overloaded and unbalanced experiences about: father / fathers / being a father.

☐ I have overloaded and unbalanced experiences about: mother / mothers / being a mother.

☐ I have overloaded and unbalanced experiences about: man / men / masculinity.

☐ I have overloaded and unbalanced experiences about: woman / women / femininity.

Comment: ....

....

....

....

....

....

....

....

....

....

....

Thesis 2

Experiences about one's own gender and the gender of the partner not only form the external masculinity (femininity), but also the inner psychical opposite gender pole. This refers to the concept of Individuation, where the inner gender pole of a man is known as "anima" and from a woman as "animus".

The more unbalanced the experiences about men and women are, the more unbalanced their inner image is (= anima, animus). With that the development of a person as a man / a woman becomes unbalanced as well.

A mature man (and a mature woman) have integrated the female (and the male) concept in polarity to an integrative wholeness. Creating this balanced wholeness is the essential characteristic of a marriage (a firm relationship) between man and woman.

Exercise 2A

Experiences of the male concept. Mark where you have not had positive experiences (or have made negative experiences) with / about men:

- ☐ Spirit as the inner guidance power and source of human values.
- ☐ Developing structures as a basic pattern for living.
- ☐ Sketch projects to realize being and life.
- ☐ Management as a centralizing force in realizing life.
- ☐ Orgasmic sex as a lovely integrative experience with love.
- ☐ Principles open to life as a foundation for developing life.
- ☐ Explorations and discovering as curiosity and pleasure of life.
- ☐ Creating (stimulating) incidents and new things in many situations.
- ☐ Analytical thinking to understand, transform, and act.
- ☐ Rational power to realize life as an expression of responsibility.
- ☐ Masculine body and sexuality integrated as a part of self-identity.

Comment: ....

....

....

....

....

....

© SCHELLHAMMER INSTITUTE

☐ ☑ Exercise 2B

☑ ☐ **Experiences of the female concept. Mark where you have not had positive experiences (or have made negative experiences) with / about women:**

☐ Expressing and living life as a source and expression of human values.

☐ Care as an expression of responsibility and a way of creating life.

☐ Nourishing as a law in physical and psychical areas.

☐ Protecting being and life because values of human beings lie inside.

☐ Care as an integrative way and expression of realization of life.

☐ Receiving as an enrichment, to understand and broaden the being.

☐ Romantic sex as a lovely integrative experience with love.

☐ Intuitive thinking to understand, improve, transform and act.

☐ Sensibility to penetrate in being and life, and to understand meaning.

☐ Emotional power to realize life as an expression of responsibility.

☐ Integrating female body and sexuality as a part of self-identity.

Comment: ....

....

....

Thesis 3

The polarity of masculinity and femininity is certainly established naturally in the psyche (mind); but it is also formed by the biography and the living environment through various fragments. The quality of a relationship depends decisively on the way partners deal with this polarity and form, transform and develop this polarity openly for living.

☐ ☑ Exercise 3

☑ ☐ **Mark how it is with you:**

☐ Masculinity and femininity don't mean a lot for my being and life.

☐ Creating a balance between masculinity and femininity is not important to me.

☐ I have developed only little balance with the opposite gender in my psyche.

☐ Creating masculinity and femininity is not a matter of discussion with my partner.

Comment: ....

....

....

Thesis 4

The whole person is at all times acting in a relationship. Both have not well formed masculine and feminine ways of expression. Without a conscious self-education, man and woman mostly have very unbalanced character traits.

Exercise 4

Mark your weaknesses / your unbalanced state:

Mark what concerns you / what is important to you: **1 = not 2 = little 3 = quite a lot 4 = a lot 5 = totally**

1	2	3	4	5	
☐	☐	☐	☐	☐	Introversion and Extraversion
☐	☐	☐	☐	☐	Striving for power and dominance
☐	☐	☐	☐	☐	Feelings of inferiority, fears (anxiety), depression
☐	☐	☐	☐	☐	Exaggerated attitude for order
☐	☐	☐	☐	☐	Excessively underlined narcissism
☐	☐	☐	☐	☐	Moods, extreme variation of temper
☐	☐	☐	☐	☐	Laziness, indifference
☐	☐	☐	☐	☐	Nagging, criticizing, condemning judgments
☐	☐	☐	☐	☐	Order in housekeeping; correctness in behavior
☐	☐	☐	☐	☐	Distribution of roles and work
☐	☐	☐	☐	☐	Sexual experiencing and acting, rejecting sexual pleasure
☐	☐	☐	☐	☐	Faithfulness and adultery; jealousy.
☐	☐	☐	☐	☐	Male and female emancipation
☐	☐	☐	☐	☐	Adaptation and creative new forming
☐	☐	☐	☐	☐	Need of autonomy and liberty

Comment: ....
....
....
....

Exercise 5
My most important problems with masculinity and femininity are:

Exercise 6
My way of better finding my polarity of masculinity and femininity:

Re-discovery of Being a Woman / Being a Man

A man and a woman living together, decided as a common course for life, is one of the most valuable kinds of living. The institution 'marriage' is created culturally for that. This isn't the same as a homosexual or a lesbian partnership.

Man and woman differ not only biologically (sexual) and through educational influences. The psychic life as a wholeness 'functions' differently. Masculine and feminine roles are not merely a product of learning processes.

Masculinity and femininity exist as a quality. That is linked psychically and physically, although in many ways deformable and in mutual action. Many marriages fail and are really 'ill' because they are thoroughly destructive and function with masks (lies). This fact doesn't speak against the high value of the institution 'marriage', of man and woman living together. Here is a great lack of self-education.

A man has to know: a man isn't a woman! A woman should have in her eye: he is a man! It is a life challenge to search, to discover and to integrate this into the psychical-spiritual life; and this not only as a matter of sexual difference! The matriarchal and patriarchal symbols are to be overcome. We have to find the truthful covered archetypes.

The genuine feminine image is the creative principle of life, the donator and preserver of life. The divine mother and the love-divinity are highest representations of femininity. Men are socialized for violence, strength, destruction, indigence of feelings, as the conquerors, maker etc.

What could be his genuine image? He also can (paternally) be as caring as a woman can think rationally. He also should have feelings like a woman. Without speaking in clichés, procreating of life, of 'projects' and managing these is an aspect of masculinity.

Perhaps it is like this: Spirit is masculine and life is a genuine feminine force (of life). Certainly man and woman have both these forces inside. Masculine and feminine forces are different, but not in their value. Both can live only with and through the other.

All actions, in private life as in social life and in the spirituality, can occur in partnership-like interests and tendency. Also a woman can be a priest, a general director or a state president; she doesn't have to become 'male' for that. On the other hand a man can be creative in household work as well in education and in forming daily life, without being 'female'.

ESSENTIAL:

1. Man and woman can bring forward evolutionary terrestrial life only with solidarity and cooperation, if both realize the inner evolution.

2. This applies to matrimonial life as well as political-economical and social life.

You want to know more, more examples and more practical ideas to this unit.
These books from Dr. Edward Schellhammer guide you for much more:

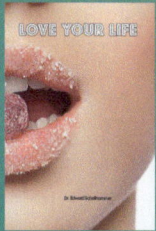

Love your Life

The Future in your Hands

Become a strong Personality

60 Days to Paradise

Practical Psychology

Love and love yourself completely

www.schellhammerinstitute.com

© SCHELLHAMMER INSTITUTE

Thesis 1

If the partner is the opposite pole in the relationship between a man and a woman, wholeness is created in the person and in the relationship. The psychological compatibility and accommodating spirit of both partners are another part of this wholeness of a person and relationship. Furthermore, love wants to realize the being, meaning of life and aims of life as a common life project.

Exercise 1

Real love between man and woman in daily life. Discover your strengths and weaknesses. Mark where you see your own weaknesses:

- ☐ Highly estimate the truthfulness of both partners.
- ☐ Promote mutual care (forming) of the psychical life.
- ☐ Turn towards emotions and interpret these feelings as an important message.
- ☐ Face the facts of life with responsibility and awareness.
- ☐ Develop (realize) the potentials and promote them with the partner.
- ☐ Value sensuality and express it in diverse ways with the partner.
- ☐ Take arguments seriously and reduce them; reconcile the same day.
- ☐ Often wanting constructive talks even with small daily matters.
- ☐ Giving high importance to psychical-spiritual growth and mutually promoting it.
- ☐ Giving certain deepness to one's own life and as well to the relationship.
- ☐ Being cautious with the own destructive forces of the unconscious.
- ☐ Not suppressing drive and desire; see the seriousness and talk about it.
- ☐ Respecting physical needs (health) and taking care of them.
- ☐ Experiencing life time as something valuable and using it in meaningful ways.
- ☐ Protecting and promoting the values of being and living together.
- ☐ Adapting a lot of knowledge to creating human life with competences (skills).
- ☐ Transforming rigid principles and norms in open patterns for life.
- ☐ Strengthening decisiveness against everything which could destroy love and truthfulness.
- ☐ Developing pleasure in discovering the inner transcendental realities.

Comment: ....
....
....
....
....

Thesis 2

Self-love is the beginning of any love. Love has to do with having interest, caring, dedicating, promoting, growing, protecting and strengthening. Love begins with turning towards psychical life and integrating it. Forming and protecting one's own life is self-love.

Exercise 2
To strengthen for love.

Mark what concerns you / what is important to you: **1 = not 2 = little 3 = quite a lot 4 = a lot 5 = totally**

1	2	3	4	5	
☐	☐	☐	☐	☐	I am interested in my inner and in my whole life.
☐	☐	☐	☐	☐	I turn consciously and critically towards what I am and live.
☐	☐	☐	☐	☐	I promote and use my potentials, tendencies and talents.
☐	☐	☐	☐	☐	I develop my weaknesses and not well formed forces.
☐	☐	☐	☐	☐	I transform my life forces and life plans into realities.
☐	☐	☐	☐	☐	I form what is not formed; I also further develop my psychical life.
☐	☐	☐	☐	☐	I control myself consciously and am balanced in my daily life.
☐	☐	☐	☐	☐	I strengthen my weaknesses; I am regardful with my limits.
☐	☐	☐	☐	☐	I give importance to my dreams, intuitions and body experiences.
☐	☐	☐	☐	☐	I am thankful facing life for all that I can live.
☐	☐	☐	☐	☐	I feel integrated in a transcendental network.
☐	☐	☐	☐	☐	I take responsibility for my happiness and my actions.
☐	☐	☐	☐	☐	I act with competences and knowledge in my personal life.
☐	☐	☐	☐	☐	I can enjoy small things on me and in my life.

Comment: ....

....

....

....

....

© SCHELLHAMMER INSTITUTE

Thesis 3

Love between man and woman is not only a psychological matter. Love is stimulated through being addressed from the character (nature) of the other gender and through the archetypal importance of a man-woman-relationship. This kind of love promotes the superior wholeness of masculinity and femininity, psychological, physical and practical in life. With such a love man and woman shall find their own wholeness through the other gender. This unification is of deep spiritual meaning and since the beginning of history one of the highest archetypes; this means: being, path and aim are the same time. The marriage as a bond and way of living between man and woman is in that sense archetypal; that means: always valid, always a special meaning of human beings and in this orientation "holy" (means: untouchable and inextinguishable value).

Exercise 3

About your relationship. Mark where you can say fully and thoroughly "Yes, that's true":

- ☐ We have some very similar character traits and qualities.
- ☐ I am a true friend to my partner when he / she is in trouble.
- ☐ In general, I feel we are very similar and we really have a lot in common.
- ☐ We can go, each his path of self-fulfillment; and nevertheless we are a whole together.
- ☐ I really feel touched how my partner realizes spiritual values of the human being.
- ☐ Our project is to find higher meaning in life; and this is our life project.
- ☐ We are very peaceful, in our sexual life as well as in all aspects of being, living and growing.
- ☐ We are like two instruments playing the same open melody of life.
- ☐ We are in our undertakings like companions and accomplices (in a good sense).
- ☐ We take the same path and within each of us his own path.
- ☐ I feel appealed from the whole nature of my partner – and my partner too.
- ☐ We can respect each other mutually in being man / woman and we experience a deep enrichment.

Comment: ....

....

....

....

....

Thesis 4

"Do you love me?" is the first question a baby asks the mother and father, even as a prenatal experience from the fetus. This implies the question after the "me", what means: "especially me; exclusively me as your child". In the relationship between man and woman this question repeats itself on another level each day; and with that often the drama from the childhood.

Exercise 4

The complete love between man and woman is a quality both have to elaborate, to work on; is never given naturally. Complete love is an essential aim of marriage.

Mark and weight what concerns you: **1** = not **2** = little **3** = quite a lot **4** = a lot **5** = totally

1 2 3 4 5

☐ ☐ ☐ ☐ ☐ I love my partner with heart, body, mind, spirit and soul.
☐ ☐ ☐ ☐ ☐ I love my partner from the bottom of my being.
☐ ☐ ☐ ☐ ☐ I love my partner with knowledge, wisdom and skills.
☐ ☐ ☐ ☐ ☐ I love my partner will full trust and faith.
☐ ☐ ☐ ☐ ☐ I love my partner with intelligence, reason, intuition, body feelings.
☐ ☐ ☐ ☐ ☐ I love my partner without "secret" reserve and unlimitedly.

Comment: ....
....
....

Exercise 5

My love for my partner has some weaknesses:

....
....
....
....

Exercise 6

I want to stimulate and deepen my love for my partner as follows:

....
....
....
....

The Openness for Self-knowledge

Self-knowledge is the starting point of every evolutionary way of life. Without self-knowledge the human being remains an 'archaic being', trapped in unconsciousness and inner chaos.

Most people don't know what to do with their dreams. Beyond certain psychological schools, publicity and political manipulation, the unconscious hasn't got any practical significance. Nobody is interested in it. Everyone 'somehow' tries to cope with their feelings and needs.

Only very few people make an effort towards methodical relaxation; most they rarely even question the level of their tensions.

Not many occupy themselves with how they perceive, think and speak. That people reject and suppress is rarely noticed.

The entire psychical life is only taught in fragmented pieces in primary education. Life will be the 'school' for adults, so they say. In life one learns: greed and envy, hatred and aggression, lies and masquerades, running the gauntlet and power strategies.

The one, who doesn't want to know anything about 'Psychology' and 'Personality Education', will hardly find access to self-knowledge.

The standard reactions are: *'I know myself well enough'*, or *'I am already developed'*, or *'nobody has got to tell me anything'*, or *'I have had enough teaching'*, or *'it is written in the Bible, how human beings have to live'*, or *'I believe in God, that's enough'*, or *'I am modest and don't want any wisdom'*, or *'stop bothering me with that rubbish'*, or *'Being rich, one lives easier'*. Again and again people have all kinds of reactions to the subject 'self-knowledge'.

If financial problems start in the married life, love and spirit quickly go away. For millions of people life is a fight for economic survival. What will self-knowledge achieve here? Solidarity for self-knowledge rarely exists in our society.

One can't earn money with self-knowledge, can't gain prestige, and self-knowledge hardly produces lust. The positive possibilities of self-knowledge are unknown.

Self-knowledge is a directed process of self-education. Man has to want that education. He has to learn certain methods. He has to do a series of clearly defined tasks. For that also some constructive attitudes are needed.

Those seeking self-knowledge, do so if they can see a gain in it – external, internal or spiritual. The one, who practices self-knowledge, appreciates higher inner values. The one who values his life higher than gadgets, goods or money, can build up an interest in his inner life.

1. Self-knowledge is an inner experience and not just cheap blabber.

2. How can you study Psychology and ignore the relevance for you?

You want to know more, more examples and more practical ideas to this unit.
These books from Dr. Edward Schellhammer guide you for much more:

Love your Life

The Future in your Hands

Become a strong Personality

60 Days to Paradise

Practical Psychology

Lesson 4

Enjoy making love with creativity

© SCHELLHAMMER INSTITUTE

Thesis 1

A human being is more than an apparatus of biological desire. A human being is also a psychical-spiritual nature. Many people mix up sexual desire with love; they think if they possess and satisfy each other physically and if they live together peacefully, they love each other.

Exercise 1

Search your weaknesses, deficits and unsatisfied needs.
Mark where you feel addressed and feel a need of changes.

Mark where you feel a need of change: **1** = not **2** = little **3** = quite a lot **4** = a lot **5** = totally

1 2 3 4 5

☐ ☐ ☐ ☐ ☐ I feel alienated from my partner in the sexual unification.

☐ ☐ ☐ ☐ ☐ Tenderness comes off the one losing out.

☐ ☐ ☐ ☐ ☐ I do not recognize my partner as a man (a woman).

☐ ☐ ☐ ☐ ☐ I only experience my partner in sexuality on a physical level.

☐ ☐ ☐ ☐ ☐ I have the impression that I am a sexual object for my partner.

☐ ☐ ☐ ☐ ☐ I think the orgasm is the purpose and aim of making love.

☐ ☐ ☐ ☐ ☐ We don't try to stimulate lust (seduce) and to increase it creatively.

☐ ☐ ☐ ☐ ☐ I don't like the moment of excitement; I feel rather embarrassed.

☐ ☐ ☐ ☐ ☐ For us "Sex = Sex". Love doesn't play an essential role.

☐ ☐ ☐ ☐ ☐ I have difficulty getting sexual satisfaction; I don't feel comfortable.

☐ ☐ ☐ ☐ ☐ We rarely create an erotic phase before we have sex.

Comment: ....

....

....

....

....

....

....

....

Thesis 2

Sexuality is interesting from the beginning of the childhood; during the whole youth till the adult age, sexuality plays an extremely important role, as a specific issue (just "sex"). Sexuality is also a part in forming the self-identity. In adult age, sex plays nearly a daily role as desire, wish, conflict, and the power of living.

Sexuality is much more than creating lust and orgasm. Accepting sexuality means accepting the nature of the human being with all possibilities of sensual experiences. If somebody really likes sex, he creates a sexual encounter with self-reflection and communication with his partner. Sexuality and eroticism regularly need creative expressions; and also contemplating and searching one's self and the partner. All sexual problems (as long as they are not medical) have to do with the whole person!

☑ Exercise 2A
The sexual biography is the foundation of the actually lived sexuality.
Mark what concerns you partly or fully:

- ☐ During my puberty sexuality was greatly overcharged with problems.
- ☐ I didn't feel comfortable during my first love relationship.
- ☐ Experiencing lust and sex was often (mostly) mixed with feelings of guilt.
- ☐ I had (still have / have) special sexual difficulties.
- ☐ My first sexual experiences were totally not pleasant.
- ☐ In my previous relationship(s) I had very embarrassing sexual moments.
- ☐ My previous failing of a love relationship also had to do with sex.
- ☐ My (religious) education concerning sex was extremely hostile towards lust.
- ☐ My previous partner(s) had serious sexual difficulties.
- ☐ I had / have feelings of inferiority in the context with sex.
- ☐ I often felt humiliated during sex, depreciated and put down.

Comment: ....

....

....

....

....

....

....

....

....

☐ ☑ **Exercise 2B**
☑ ☐   **Attitudes. Put a cross where you feel partly or fully concerned.**

☐   I don't have a relaxed positive attitude about sexuality.

☐   I don't have a relaxed positive attitude about menstruation.

☐   I don't have a relaxed positive attitude about ejaculation.

☐   I don't have a relaxed positive attitude about orgasm.

☐   I don't have a relaxed positive attitude about physical release.

☐   I don't have a relaxed positive attitude about (erected) penis.

☐   I don't have a relaxed positive attitude about (wet) vagina.

☐   I don't have a relaxed positive attitude about breasts and nipples.

☐   I don't have a relaxed positive attitude about my strongly excited partner.

☐   I don't have a relaxed positive attitude about passionate oral sex.

☐   I don't have a relaxed positive attitude about seducing my partner.

☐   I don't have a relaxed positive attitude about sexual manifold creativity.

Comment: ....

....

....

....

....

....

....

....

....

....

....

....

Thesis 3 — A human being with his psychical-spiritual wholeness always contributes much more to the sexual play than a simple sexual act. For example: The initiation phase is more than increasing lust, it is a human encounter! Being naked produces more than just lust, it often means being unprotected, sometimes even fear of being punished, or simply complete dedication.

Exercise 3
Sex and experiences as a human being.

Mark what concerns you: 1 = not 2 = little 3 = quite a lot 4 = a lot 5 = totally

1 2 3 4 5

☐ ☐ ☐ ☐ ☐ Whilst experiencing sex I feel vulnerable, sensitive, easily offended.

☐ ☐ ☐ ☐ ☐ The sexual encounter produces fear, shame and embarrassment.

☐ ☐ ☐ ☐ ☐ I feel inner closure, blockage, things from the day or sorrow.

☐ ☐ ☐ ☐ ☐ I have a strong self-control; I feel observed when I have sex.

☐ ☐ ☐ ☐ ☐ I doubt myself, feelings of inferiority (physical appearance).

☐ ☐ ☐ ☐ ☐ I have fear that the problems from the past will repeat themselves.

☐ ☐ ☐ ☐ ☐ I feel pressure to perform, fear of not being good enough.

☐ ☐ ☐ ☐ ☐ I feel restraint to tell my partner when I want sex.

☐ ☐ ☐ ☐ ☐ I don't feel well with the shape and size of my penis / my breasts.

Comment: ....

....

....

Thesis 4 — Sexual experience and acting also includes communication; real words or messages expressed in tenderness, kisses, chatting, touching, or making eye contact. Therefore, sexuality is also a complete sensual experience and forms the self-identity of a person. Symbolic expressions and words during the sexual act move the whole person and not simply the body!

Exercise 4
Messages to the love game.
Mark what you miss partly or entirely from your partner when you make love:

- [ ] How do you feel that? Do you like that? Does this annoy you?
- [ ] What do you like? Show me how you like it!
- [ ] What / how do you want to do it now? What increases your lust?
- [ ] Take your time! It's wonderful to be with you now in that way.
- [ ] I would like to try something new. You too?
- [ ] What do you like especially on me?
- [ ] I love you, your body, and the way you are, also when we have sex.
- [ ] Tell me if you don't like something, if something inconveniences you.

Comment: ....
....
....
....

Exercise 5
What I miss when having sex on the level of love:

....
....
....
....

Exercise 6
On the level of the sexual act I have problems with:

1. ....   4. ....
2. ....   5. ....
3. ....   6. ....

Exercise 7
What I sometimes want my partner to say when making love:

....
....
....
....

To Love Sexuality

Sexual lust is today certainly more accepted than 20 years ago. Many people can live with intimate tenderness, intercourse and masturbation free of hostile moralizing and attitudes to life. But more: Sex-supermarket and sex-services of all kinds are expanding more than ever. Some offers may be helpful, also for learning. But many of these hinder man and woman to profoundly love sexuality.

In sexual life everything is allowed, some say; others experience sexuality with vulnerability, with most intimate sensibility, with values and limits. Reproduction is one aspect. Self-experience, lust, relaxation and intimate experiences of the partner allow a deep, enriching acceptance of life. Consumption and 'free love' seems to break all limits; a reaction against centuries-old hostile attitudes towards sexuality!

In earlier times sexuality was burdened with guilt and shame. Lust and joy are today in unlimited expansion. Is that 'bad'? Human beings satisfy themselves with eating, drinking and with sweets, cars, clothes, amusements or

TO LOVE SEXUALITY MEANS THEREFORE: TO LOVE ONESELF AND THE OTHER.

a foam bath and much more. A wide sensual experience has become a daily aim.

Bodily experiences and sensuality are a central part of our life.

The main question is not *"How much sexual satisfaction alone or with others is still 'healthy' (not-neurotic)?"*, but rather: *"How can the human being live his sexual satisfaction constructively and in a fulfilling way?"*

In the sexual experience we are sensitive, intimately touched and vulnerable, either lacking a partner or confronted with a partner. Everybody is required to say 'yes' to himself, to his experience and actions; to integrate his needs in his identity and to create his fulfillment of happiness with delight. That is

more than 'sexual relaxation'. This is 'self-discovering', encountering oneself and the other, devotion and self-relation. This can be done mechanistically, creatively and with love.

Without the ability of enjoyment, lust isn't fulfilling happiness. But how could happiness be, if in the sexual life only stimulus with lust and not the human being are at the centre of experience and action?

The fast reaction of a lust-experience under the blanket is

not a loving sexual practice; it may be comparable with a hasty bite of a dry, cold hamburger. A tender contact is more than sensing of touch and skin.

Tenderness is a symbolic action. It contains a message to 'you', and it contains the experience of the response. It is similar with all variants of sexual plays. They inform the partner about something and they are an experience of the effects, bodily, psychically and spiritually.

You want to know more, more examples and more practical ideas to this unit. These books from Dr. Edward Schellhammer guide you for much more:

Love your Life

The Future in your Hands

Become a strong Personality

60 Days to Paradise

Practical Psychology

Lesson 5

Live your relationship partnership-like

© SCHELLHAMMER INSTITUTE

Thesis 1 — There are several possible attempts to avoid arising arguments and conflicts in a love relationship; or to deal with such situations constructively. Both partners jointly determine the conditions and rules for a constructive living together and for a constructive dealing with life matters.

Exercise 1
Search your weaknesses, deficits and needs.
Mark where you see deficits for yourself and for your relationship.

- Continuous effort to understand oneself and the partner.
- Regularly see the partner in new ways in his being and growing.
- Continuously explain in one's own being and growing.
- Mutually promoting and developing being a man / a woman.
- Elaborating and revising the basic values together.
- To understand self-management in daily life as a matter of both.
- Creating a home to feel comfortable and where each one has his own place.
- Regularly creating common experiences that produce joy.
- Regularly finding agreements in all matters, also in petty matters.
- To understand and elaborate the common biography of the relationship.
- Forming a couple-identity through the common biography.
- Respecting the fact that both are in permanent development as a personality.
- Continuously learning about psyche, love, emotions, and sex.
- In all areas always promote and use creativity.
- Arguing correctly without games of rejection or blocking each other.
- Not mutually balancing the mistakes. To forgive and to reconcile!
- Reducing life lies without reproaching each other; and learning from that.
- Dealing seriously with one's own dreams.
- Giving higher importance to the psychical-spiritual life than to external values.
- Each one practices self-education and personal development (= Individuation) in his own way.

Comment: ....
....
....
....
....

Thesis 2

In a dialogue there are realities which need to be accepted, for example: A complete accord is rarely possible. Talking about talking promotes understanding. One cannot talk better than one perceives, thinks, and has knowledge. Talking is always an expression of a previous thinking and feeling. Communication is a very important way of dealing with realities. Communication is always more human oriented than object-oriented.

Exercise 2
Our communication (talks) proceeds / is:

Mark what concerns you: **1 = not 2 = little 3 = quite a lot 4 = a lot 5 = totally**

1	2	3	4	5	
☐	☐	☐	☐	☐	objectives, informative, precise
☐	☐	☐	☐	☐	transparent, open, not hiding
☐	☐	☐	☐	☐	cooperative, partnership-like
☐	☐	☐	☐	☐	conscious, profound, binding
☐	☐	☐	☐	☐	efficient in time use, organized, systematic
☐	☐	☐	☐	☐	asking, adapting actively and flexibly
☐	☐	☐	☐	☐	prudent, serious, tranquil, decisive
☐	☐	☐	☐	☐	concentrated, conscious, listening well
☐	☐	☐	☐	☐	planned, settled, prepared

Comment: ....

....

....

....

....

....

....

....

....

....

Thesis 3

Arguments and conflicts can be avoided or reduced by practical actions. The way a person faces a problem talking to his partner is often more important than the problem (conflict) itself.

Exercise 3
How do you treat your partner?
Mark where you see a deficit for yourself and your relationship:

☐ friendly, obliging, benevolent, courteous, respectful

☐ honest, authentic, open, without games, fair, just, not ignoring

☐ flexible and adapting style (language, behavior) and issue (matter)

☐ democratic, partnership-like, cooperative, supportive, tied-up

Comment:

....
....
....
....
....
....
....
....
....
....
....
....
....
....

Thesis 4

Practical rules of behavior and communication are embedded in a whole complex:

- Accepting the complexity of the psyche (mind), of the psychical-spiritual growth, and of the realities of life.

- Finding and understanding continuously one's self and the partner in the genuine whole being and growing anew.

- Accepting and promoting mutual self-education and life learning.

- A well functioning relationship is based decisively on the forming of the psychical functions (self-education and life learning).

- Self-education doesn't make the relationship good; love is ultimately decisive.

- Love without life learning and without using intelligence destroys itself.

☑ Exercise 4
☑ 12 rules of partnership-like communication.
Mark where you see deficits for yourself and for your relationship:

- ☐ Not humiliating, not hurting, not depreciating, and not mocking.
- ☐ Not interposing, not exaggerating, and not losing the tone.
- ☐ Discussing matters cooperatively, mutually, complementarily, and together.
- ☐ Communication: plain, clear, objective, differentiated, open, direct.
- ☐ Listening, understanding, giving weight, selecting, letting the partner articulate.
- ☐ Adequately expressing problems, wishes, questions and feelings.
- ☐ Holding and allowing distance and autonomy.
- ☐ Respect for the partner as an autonomous person.
- ☐ Considering spiritual bonds (e.g. dreams), intuition and inner resonance.
- ☐ Considering physical state of oneself and of the partner.
- ☐ Understanding the past as a challenge for learning, and not as a reproach.
- ☐ Continuously thinking and renewing values, norms and attitudes.

Comment: ....

....

....

....

Lets be "human":

Misunderstandings are normal. Conflicts and arguments are part of life. Infringing the rules of good communication and of appropriate conducts is human (but should not become a habit!).

Exercise 5
I recognize a deficit in my way of creating relationships:

....

....

....

....

....

....

....

Exercise 6
I will talk to my partner about what we can improve, for example:

....

....

....

....

....

....

....

....

....

....

....

Love Being on this Earth

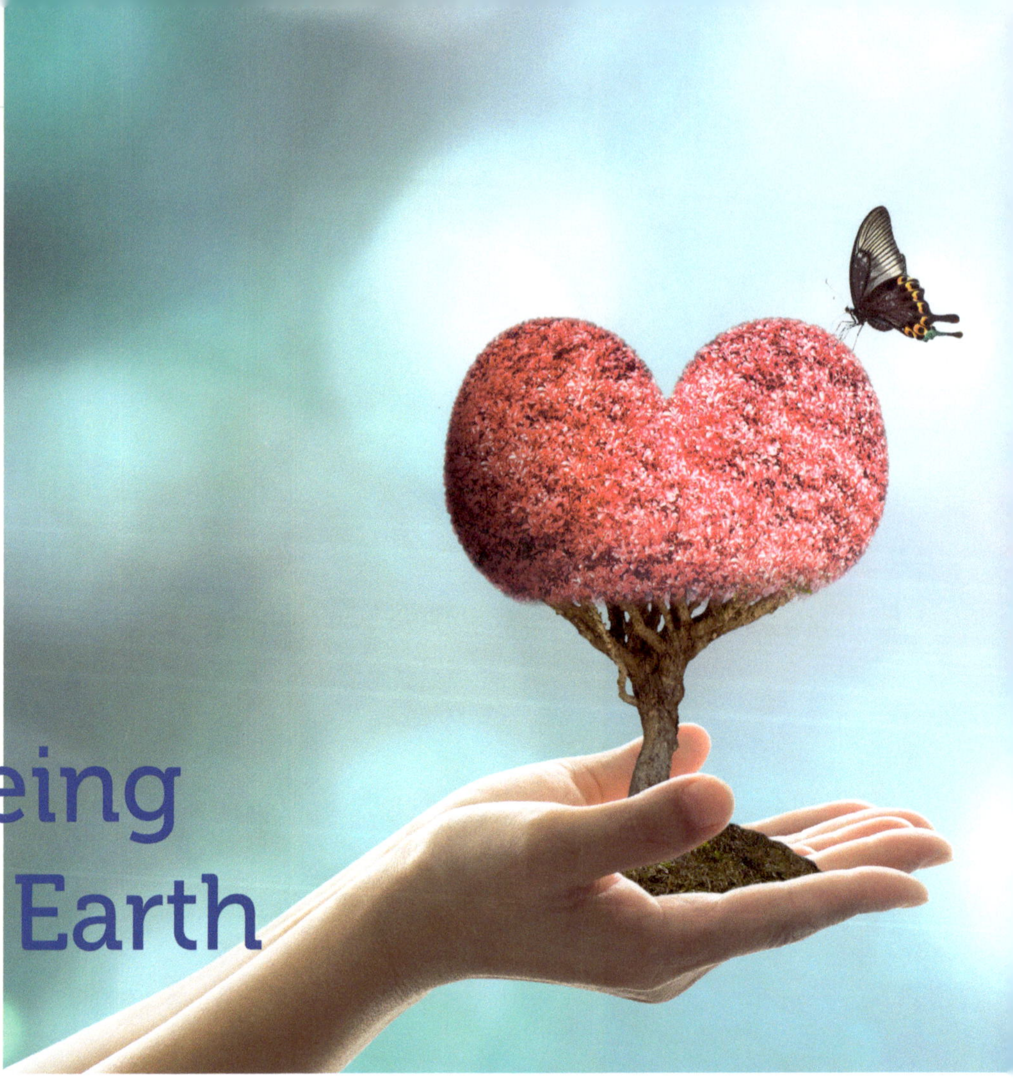

Value your physical being, your psychological being, your talents, your special character, and your spiritual potentials.

Value everything life offers you to live and to realize yourself, including all the small things that can make you enjoy life.

Value all possibilities to learn for your development, for your work, for your home, for your life with a partner, for a relationship and for a family.

Value what your society can give you: a frame for your life, infrastructure, a cultural identity, and much more.

Value the history of your country and culture with all the countless efforts made for a better and more comfortable life during centuries by all the pioneers.

LOVE IS FOR:
yourself, your partner,
your children, the world of
children and adolescents,
the world of adults and
elderly people, humanity
and the earth (nature),
the inner Spirit and God.

Abilities to love are expressed in:

- Having an active interest in the psychical-spiritual life of humans.

- Giving high importance to one's own psychical-spiritual life.

- Consciously forming the entire psychical inner life.

- Valuing, promoting and using one's own real resources.

- Contemplating about the high values of human beings.

- Discovering spirituality inside oneself and in other people.

- Being vigilant with the destructive forces of the unconscious.

- Caring for constructive and many-sided thinking and acting.

- Being open to live one's own desires in a creative way.

- Respecting the healthy needs of the body and taking care of them.

- Regularly and actively experiencing nature and valuing it.

- Protecting and caring for the values of family and relationship.

You want to know more, more examples and more practical ideas to this unit.
These books from Dr. Edward Schellhammer guide you for much more:

Love your Life

The Future in your Hands

Become a strong Personality

60 Days to Paradise

Practical Psychology

Prepare yourself well for love

1. You want to renew your actual relationship. Elaborate the following exercises and show the result to your partner! After that your partner shall do the same and present you their result.

2. You want a new start. You are looking for a partner. You want an ambitious relationship. Elaborating these exercises, you prepare yourself for that. Looking for a partner comes later and especially when making the decision for a partner!

© SCHELLHAMMER INSTITUTE

Thesis 1

The way of living forms in the common frame in which a life with a partner develops.

Exercise 1
I see my way of living in general as follows:

Mark what concerns you: 1 = not 2 = little 3 = quite a lot 4 = a lot 5 = totally

1	2	3	4	5		1	2	3	4	5	
☐	☐	☐	☐	☐	Doing active sport	☐	☐	☐	☐	☐	Consumption of alcohol
☐	☐	☐	☐	☐	Smoker	☐	☐	☐	☐	☐	Watching television
☐	☐	☐	☐	☐	Traveling	☐	☐	☐	☐	☐	I like cooking
☐	☐	☐	☐	☐	Going to bars	☐	☐	☐	☐	☐	Concerts/theatre
☐	☐	☐	☐	☐	Like discos	☐	☐	☐	☐	☐	Aesthete, with style
☐	☐	☐	☐	☐	Social type	☐	☐	☐	☐	☐	Circle of friends
☐	☐	☐	☐	☐	Fashion-oriented	☐	☐	☐	☐	☐	Comfortable clothing
☐	☐	☐	☐	☐	Energetic type	☐	☐	☐	☐	☐	Practical type
☐	☐	☐	☐	☐	Intellectual type	☐	☐	☐	☐	☐	Artist type
☐	☐	☐	☐	☐	Business type	☐	☐	☐	☐	☐	Caring type
☐	☐	☐	☐	☐	Individualist type	☐	☐	☐	☐	☐	Suit of clothes type
☐	☐	☐	☐	☐	I like nature	☐	☐	☐	☐	☐	Animal lover

Comment: ....

....

....

....

....

....

....

Thesis 1 — Each person can develop himself; determine his paths and aims with autonomy. Or ignore and reject. The level and the way of creating this kind of self-forming forms the quality of a relationship.

Exercise 2
I see <u>myself as a person</u> and my nature in the following way:

Mark what is important to you: **1 = not 2 = little 3 = quite a lot 4 = a lot 5 = totally**

1	2	3	4	5		1	2	3	4	5	
☐	☐	☐	☐	☐	Experienced in life	☐	☐	☐	☐	☐	Self-strong
☐	☐	☐	☐	☐	Peaceful	☐	☐	☐	☐	☐	Well-read
☐	☐	☐	☐	☐	Optimistic	☐	☐	☐	☐	☐	Mentally awake
☐	☐	☐	☐	☐	Enterprising	☐	☐	☐	☐	☐	Sympathetic ability
☐	☐	☐	☐	☐	Thoughtful	☐	☐	☐	☐	☐	Sympathetic mind
☐	☐	☐	☐	☐	Flexible	☐	☐	☐	☐	☐	Caring
☐	☐	☐	☐	☐	Self-critical	☐	☐	☐	☐	☐	Unique
☐	☐	☐	☐	☐	Self-assured	☐	☐	☐	☐	☐	Reliable
☐	☐	☐	☐	☐	Tolerant	☐	☐	☐	☐	☐	Well cared
☐	☐	☐	☐	☐	Cheerful-vital	☐	☐	☐	☐	☐	Honest
☐	☐	☐	☐	☐	Sensible	☐	☐	☐	☐	☐	Faithful, loyal
☐	☐	☐	☐	☐	Generous	☐	☐	☐	☐	☐	Lovely
☐	☐	☐	☐	☐	Contemplative	☐	☐	☐	☐	☐	Authentic
☐	☐	☐	☐	☐	Independent	☐	☐	☐	☐	☐	Transparent
☐	☐	☐	☐	☐	Stable	☐	☐	☐	☐	☐	Humorous
☐	☐	☐	☐	☐	Attentive	☐	☐	☐	☐	☐	Pragmatic
☐	☐	☐	☐	☐	Vigilant	☐	☐	☐	☐	☐	Serious-minded
☐	☐	☐	☐	☐	Free-spirited	☐	☐	☐	☐	☐	With a clear life path
☐	☐	☐	☐	☐	Self-confident	☐	☐	☐	☐	☐	Able to love
☐	☐	☐	☐	☐	Decisive	☐	☐	☐	☐	☐	Free in my inner life
☐	☐	☐	☐	☐	Intuitive	☐	☐	☐	☐	☐	Passionate
☐	☐	☐	☐	☐	Balanced	☐	☐	☐	☐	☐	Ambitious

1	2	3	4	5	
☐	☐	☐	☐	☐	Educated
☐	☐	☐	☐	☐	Kind-hearted
☐	☐	☐	☐	☐	Easy going
☐	☐	☐	☐	☐	Purposeful
☐	☐	☐	☐	☐	Benevolent
☐	☐	☐	☐	☐	Responsible
☐	☐	☐	☐	☐	Oncoming
☐	☐	☐	☐	☐	Respectful
☐	☐	☐	☐	☐	Charismatic
☐	☐	☐	☐	☐	Open to the world
☐	☐	☐	☐	☐	Circumspect
☐	☐	☐	☐	☐	Unconstrained
☐	☐	☐	☐	☐	Creative
☐	☐	☐	☐	☐	Meaning-oriented
☐	☐	☐	☐	☐	Wise
☐	☐	☐	☐	☐	Enthusiastic
☐	☐	☐	☐	☐	Sharpened mind
☐	☐	☐	☐	☐	Spiritual
☐	☐	☐	☐	☐	Open to learn
☐	☐	☐	☐	☐	Open for life
☐	☐	☐	☐	☐	Interested

1	2	3	4	5	
☐	☐	☐	☐	☐	Open for experiments
☐	☐	☐	☐	☐	Forgiving
☐	☐	☐	☐	☐	Self-determined
☐	☐	☐	☐	☐	Communicative
☐	☐	☐	☐	☐	Autonomous
☐	☐	☐	☐	☐	Like being alone
☐	☐	☐	☐	☐	Phenomenal
☐	☐	☐	☐	☐	Exceptional
☐	☐	☐	☐	☐	Orderliness
☐	☐	☐	☐	☐	Trustworthy
☐	☐	☐	☐	☐	Full of hope
☐	☐	☐	☐	☐	Able for compromises
☐	☐	☐	☐	☐	Able to get orgasm
☐	☐	☐	☐	☐	Attentive
☐	☐	☐	☐	☐	Entertaining
☐	☐	☐	☐	☐	Hard worker
☐	☐	☐	☐	☐	Sexually natural
☐	☐	☐	☐	☐	Open to grow
☐	☐	☐	☐	☐	With life aims
☐	☐	☐	☐	☐	Understanding
☐	☐	☐	☐	☐	Charitable

Comment: ....

....

....

....

....

....

....

Exercise 3
I have the following perception about the way of living of my partner:

The actual relationship: This is how I see my partner: 1 = not 2 = little 3 = quite a lot 4 = a lot 5 = totally

1	2	3	4	5		1	2	3	4	5	
☐	☐	☐	☐	☐	Doing active sport	☐	☐	☐	☐	☐	Consumption of alcohol
☐	☐	☐	☐	☐	Smoker	☐	☐	☐	☐	☐	Watching television
☐	☐	☐	☐	☐	Traveling	☐	☐	☐	☐	☐	I like cooking
☐	☐	☐	☐	☐	Going to bars	☐	☐	☐	☐	☐	Concerts/theatre
☐	☐	☐	☐	☐	Like discos	☐	☐	☐	☐	☐	Aesthete, with style
☐	☐	☐	☐	☐	Social type	☐	☐	☐	☐	☐	Circle of friends
☐	☐	☐	☐	☐	Fashion-oriented	☐	☐	☐	☐	☐	Comfortable clothing
☐	☐	☐	☐	☐	Energetic type	☐	☐	☐	☐	☐	Practical type
☐	☐	☐	☐	☐	Intellectual type	☐	☐	☐	☐	☐	Artist type
☐	☐	☐	☐	☐	Business type	☐	☐	☐	☐	☐	Caring type
☐	☐	☐	☐	☐	Individualist type	☐	☐	☐	☐	☐	Suit of clothes type
☐	☐	☐	☐	☐	I like nature	☐	☐	☐	☐	☐	Animal lover

Comment:

....

....

....

....

 Exercise 4
I wish a partner to have the following characteristics / attributes:

Mark what is important to you: 1 = not 2 = little 3 = quite a lot 4 = a lot 5 = totally

1	2	3	4	5		1	2	3	4	5	
☐	☐	☐	☐	☐	Experienced in life	☐	☐	☐	☐	☐	Sensible
☐	☐	☐	☐	☐	Peaceful	☐	☐	☐	☐	☐	Generous
☐	☐	☐	☐	☐	Optimistic	☐	☐	☐	☐	☐	Contemplative
☐	☐	☐	☐	☐	Enterprising	☐	☐	☐	☐	☐	Independent
☐	☐	☐	☐	☐	Thoughtful	☐	☐	☐	☐	☐	Stable
☐	☐	☐	☐	☐	Flexible	☐	☐	☐	☐	☐	Attentive
☐	☐	☐	☐	☐	Self-critical	☐	☐	☐	☐	☐	Vigilant
☐	☐	☐	☐	☐	Self-assured	☐	☐	☐	☐	☐	Free-spirited
☐	☐	☐	☐	☐	Tolerant	☐	☐	☐	☐	☐	Self-confident
☐	☐	☐	☐	☐	Cheerful-vital	☐	☐	☐	☐	☐	Decisive

www.schellhammerinstitute.com
© SCHELLHAMMER INSTITUTE

1	2	3	4	5	
☐	☐	☐	☐	☐	Intuitive
☐	☐	☐	☐	☐	Balanced
☐	☐	☐	☐	☐	Self-strong
☐	☐	☐	☐	☐	Well-read
☐	☐	☐	☐	☐	Mentally awake
☐	☐	☐	☐	☐	Sympathetic ability
☐	☐	☐	☐	☐	Sympathetic mind
☐	☐	☐	☐	☐	Caring
☐	☐	☐	☐	☐	Unique
☐	☐	☐	☐	☐	Reliable
☐	☐	☐	☐	☐	Well cared
☐	☐	☐	☐	☐	Honest
☐	☐	☐	☐	☐	Faithful, loyal
☐	☐	☐	☐	☐	Lovely
☐	☐	☐	☐	☐	Authentic
☐	☐	☐	☐	☐	Transparent
☐	☐	☐	☐	☐	Humorous
☐	☐	☐	☐	☐	Pragmatic
☐	☐	☐	☐	☐	Serious-minded
☐	☐	☐	☐	☐	With a clear life path
☐	☐	☐	☐	☐	Able to love
☐	☐	☐	☐	☐	Free in my inner life
☐	☐	☐	☐	☐	Passionate
☐	☐	☐	☐	☐	Ambitious
☐	☐	☐	☐	☐	Educated
☐	☐	☐	☐	☐	Kind-hearted
☐	☐	☐	☐	☐	Easy going
☐	☐	☐	☐	☐	Purposeful
☐	☐	☐	☐	☐	Benevolent
☐	☐	☐	☐	☐	Responsible
☐	☐	☐	☐	☐	Oncoming
☐	☐	☐	☐	☐	Respectful
☐	☐	☐	☐	☐	Charismatic

1	2	3	4	5	
☐	☐	☐	☐	☐	Open to the world
☐	☐	☐	☐	☐	Circumspect
☐	☐	☐	☐	☐	Unconstrained
☐	☐	☐	☐	☐	Creative
☐	☐	☐	☐	☐	Meaning-oriented
☐	☐	☐	☐	☐	Wise
☐	☐	☐	☐	☐	Enthusiastic
☐	☐	☐	☐	☐	Sharpened mind
☐	☐	☐	☐	☐	Spiritual
☐	☐	☐	☐	☐	Open to learn
☐	☐	☐	☐	☐	Open for life
☐	☐	☐	☐	☐	Interested
☐	☐	☐	☐	☐	Open for experiments
☐	☐	☐	☐	☐	Forgiving
☐	☐	☐	☐	☐	Self-determined
☐	☐	☐	☐	☐	Communicative
☐	☐	☐	☐	☐	Autonomous
☐	☐	☐	☐	☐	Like being alone
☐	☐	☐	☐	☐	Phenomenal
☐	☐	☐	☐	☐	Exceptional
☐	☐	☐	☐	☐	Orderliness
☐	☐	☐	☐	☐	Trustworthy
☐	☐	☐	☐	☐	Full of hope
☐	☐	☐	☐	☐	Able for compromises
☐	☐	☐	☐	☐	Able to get orgasm
☐	☐	☐	☐	☐	Attentive
☐	☐	☐	☐	☐	Entertaining
☐	☐	☐	☐	☐	Hard worker
☐	☐	☐	☐	☐	Sexually natural
☐	☐	☐	☐	☐	Open to grow
☐	☐	☐	☐	☐	With life aims
☐	☐	☐	☐	☐	Understanding
☐	☐	☐	☐	☐	Charitable

Comment: ....

....

....

Exercise 5
In no way do I want my partner to have / be / do / wish:

Exercise 6
Write down 3 points about what has highest importance to you:

Characteristics of Partnership

Partnership is an ideal of a modern relationship between man and woman.

We formulate some theses from an overview of actual books on that subject:

- Partnership is not equal relationship, but contains specific characteristics.

- Mutual interest for daily reality is essential for both partners.

- Openness for the real life of both partners always also contains conflicts.

- Partners respect each other in their different being (character, gender).

- Reciprocity (reversibility) and thus equal standing are considered to be principles.

- Closeness and distance periodically, form a normal part of being together.

- The biography of each is as important as the respective identities.

- Love promotes Individuation, and thus the individual human creation.

- Partners communicate about their differences and things they have in common.

- Partnership is not a static state according to a contract, but a process.

- Partners respect the limitations of each other and the 'world' of the other.

- Partners know that limits can't be crossed at any time.

- Daily life takes up a central space, has to be organized by talking about it.

- Love in the partnership must be regularly stimulated and formed.

- Partnership regulates the common things by communication.

- The power-situation is balanced, and has to be worked at, daily.

- In the partnership the mistakes of both are not calculated.

- Self-realization (forming of the identity) implies self-devotion.

- Reason and intelligence are basic functions, but they don't guarantee love.

- Eroticism and being in love have their place in the normality of daily life.

- Partners can deal with the 'inner child' of each other.

- The parallel development of identity stands in a reciprocal dynamism.

- Both partners know: every few years the self-identity changes.

- In a partnership ego-feelings and sexual experiences are encouraged.

- Partners mutually create their femininity and masculinity.

- Also by solving objective questions both are a 'team'.

- Working out the unconscious life (the biography) is partly a shared activity.

- Partners orient themselves on their dreams, intuitions and meditations.

- Partners enrich each other mutually with creative actions during their leisure.

- In a partnership a role division can be accepted.

- To live in a partnership is strenuous and demands a qualified self-management.

- Moments of symbiotic feelings may have a place in the normality of the daily life.

- Partnership-like love isn't possible without tensions and risks.

- The partners don't 'possess' each other with their whole being.

- Seduction and lust are forces equally dynamic as objectivity.

- The mutual dependence of sexual satisfaction is not against autonomy.

- The ability to understand belongs to the ability for love; this is strenuous.

You want to know more, more examples and more practical ideas to this unit. These books from Dr. Edward Schellhammer guide you for much more:

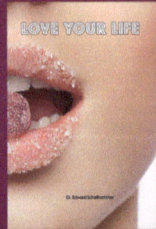

Love your Life

The Future in your Hands

Become a strong Personality

60 Days to Paradise

Practical Psychology

CERTIFICATE
of ACHIEVEMENT

SCHELLHAMMER INSTITUTE
IN SOMNIS VERITAS

Is Hereby Awarded to

Name Surname

In Recognition of Completing The Distance Learning Course:
Love Your Life; Course Program Level 1;
Course 1.1: Practice the Art to Love.

AWARDED ON   SIGNATURE

2017

Certification

Complete this distance learning program with a certification.
Contact the Schellhammer Institute to take the tests of this course unit
and collect them all to get your Diploma.

Books by Dr. Edward Schellhammer (in English)

			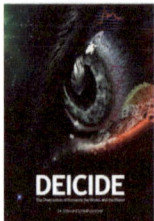			
60 Days to Paradise	Armageddon or Evolution	Become a strong Personality	Deicide	Economics I	Economics II	Economics III
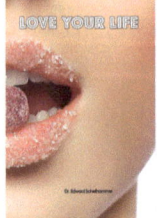	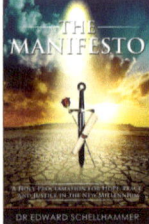			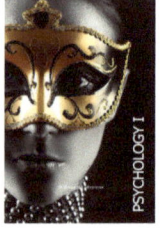		
Love your Life	The Manifesto	Politics	Practical Psychology	Psychology I	The Future in your Hands	Modern Dream Theory

Books by Dr. Edward Schellhammer (in German)

60 Tage zum Paradies	Der innere Mensch	Dialog mit dem Unbewussten	Die archetypische Mission	Die archetypischen Prozesse der Seele	Die Zukunft in deiner Hand	Evolutionäre Menschenbildung

Liebe Dein Leben	Das Manifest	Mensch-Sein in der Zukunft	Moderne Traumtheorie	Modernes Traumlexikon	Praktische Psychologie	Psychologie I

Psychologie II	Psychologie III	Theorien der Psychologie	Werde eine starke Persoenlichkeit	Jesus im Supermarkt		Books by Dr. Edward Schellhammer are Available at Amazon and Kindle

www.ingramcontent.com/pod-product-compliance
Lightning Source LLC
Chambersburg PA
CBHW041513280526
45792CB00004B/1234